*For my mom, Bernadette.*

## INTRODUCTION

'Fragile Mind' is a collection of poetry related to mental illness, that aims to achieve two key objectives:

1. To help those that suffer with the torment of mental health struggles, such as anxiety and depression; realise that they are not alone.

2. To provide non-sufferers with a window into the minds of those that struggle with a mental illness.

It is my hope that in achieving both of these objectives, 'sufferers' and 'non-sufferers' can have a stronger connection of support, understanding and patience.

With first-hand experience of mental health sufferers, including self-abusing family members and close friends that have taken their own life, a common theme has always endured. Like faith or religion, 'sufferers' share a common belief in that they are completely alone. Failing to attach to the commonality of someone that shared their torment, they believe the burden is solely theirs. They fail to believe that 'non-sufferers' understand, thinking instead that their existence is merely tolerated within borders of convenience. Eventually they isolate themselves and self-abuse, or worse.

Ironically, a significant portion of the world's population are afflicted. And as per any support group, a 'sufferer' may find comfort in knowing there are people that have exactly the same thoughts, emotions and experiences. Friends and loved ones of the 'sufferers' may finally enjoy a closer connection if they were able to empathise and sympathise with the tormenting thoughts of those in torment.   Instead of wishing and wondering what could have been done differently to help when it's too late.

So please, share in these poems with attention and emotion and delve deep into the thoughts of 'sufferers'.   And for all the afflicted that completely relate, then my message to you is - *"You're Not Alone"*.

Reach out.  Seek help.

Survive...


# 2017 SUICIDE STATISTICS

Mental Health related illnesses are having a devastating effect on society, as more and more people are taking their own life following mental health battles.  Below are some disturbing suicide statistics from the United Kingdom and United States:

## UK Statistics

- The Mental Health Foundation reported that in 2017, **suicide was the most common cause for death for men aged 20-49** in England and Wales.

- **5,821 suicides** were recorded in Great Britain, 75% were male and 25% were female.  That is **one death by suicide every two hours**.

- **Suicide is the leading cause of death among young people** aged 20-34 in the UK.

- Between 2003 and 2013, **18,220 people with mental health problem**

**took their own life**.

- **Men are less likely than women to ask for help** or talk about depression or suicidal feelings.

- Only 27% of people who died by suicide between 2005 and 2015 had been in contact with mental health services in the year before they died.

- A 2014 Psychiatric Morbidity Survey highlighted that, every week, **1 in 6 adults experiences a common mental health problem**, such as anxiety or depression; and **1 in 5 adults has considered taking their own life** at some point.

## US Statistics

- **Suicide was the 10th leading cause of death** overall in the United States in 2017. **47,000 took their own life**.

- Suicide is the **2ⁿᵈ leading cause of death** among individuals between the ages of **10 and 34**; and the **4ᵗʰ leading cause of death** among individuals between the ages of **35 and 54**

- There were more than **twice as many suicides** (47,173) in the United States **as there were homicides** (19,510)

- Between 2001 and 2017, the **total suicide rate increased 31%**

- The suicide rate among **males remained four times higher** than among females

- Across all age groups, **suicide attempts were highest among adults aged 18-25**

# FRAGILE MIND

By W.B. THOMPSON

# THE FRAGILE MIND

The fragile mind, a step behind,
Sanity, insanity intertwined;
Thoughts loose, self-abuse,
Oh my mind, please be kind.

A futile plea, not to be,
A functioning soul in society;
It's not my choice, a silent voice,
Lost within the echoes.

Behind the skin, they look within,
Twisted chaos of charity and sin;
Who do they see?
For sure not me,

All they find, is my fragile mind.

# MIRROR MAN

I wonder what you see
Mirror man of me

I envy at your smile
So confident and sure
Loved by all around you
Championed and adored

Shoulders that are steady
A family perched atop
Convictions at the ready
Resilience evermore

Oh to be you, mirror man
What a dream it must be
But when you look back mirror man
What is it you see
Tell me fearsome mirror man
Mirror man of me.

# JUST CAN'T SAY

I just can't say my thoughts today,
They'd frighten all my friends away;
Instead I smile and after a while,
These thoughts corrode my being.

The darkness of a hollow soul,
Impervious to light;
Sunken into an endless hole,
Ready to give up the fight.

I just can't say my thoughts today,
I wish tomorrow would go away.

# THE CHAMELEON

My colours ever-changing,
To blend into the crowd;
Fake smiles never fading,
Eternal sorrows not allowed.

I hide at a sense of danger,
Someone getting close;
My shine a little faded,
Shrouded in a cloak.

Ever clutching to my mind's branch,
For fear I'll one day fall;
The constant knowing of a chance,
One day I'll lose it all.

Maybe we'll become extinct,
Pained souls like you and I;
Till then I'll keep changing colour,
My way of getting by.

# BOTTLED UP

My Soul,
Bottled with a cork,
Designed to keep everything inside.
Fizzing with pressure,
Ready to explode,
Contents released,
Spilling emotion,
Consumed by those around.

# IMMITATION

I watch the world pass me by,
Like a movie that I'm not in,
Full of characters I don't know,
Nor do they know that I'm there,
The real face behind the lens.

I try and emulate their emotions,
Joy, laughter, sorrow, pain;
But the soul is numbed, unable to feel.

A failed immitation of existence.

# ROUNDABOUT

Bound to life's cruel roundabout,
Spun and dizzied;
Scared of falling into the world,
To be pulled down by the clutching hands of expectation.

Nauseous,
But committed to suffer the ride;
A repetition of blurred pain,
An endless cycle of torment.

Just one step away from salvation,
One step,
And the world would stop spinning.

# AUTO PILOT

My auto pilot did it's job well today,
It smiled when it needed to smile,
Laughed when it needed to laugh,
And I, a seemingly model of contentedness.

It raised me from my bed,
A dark slumber of which I would normally sink,
It carried me to work,
And I inside the cabin, protected from ambience and stresses.

I don't recall what it said,
But people responded well,
An illusion of friendship,
And I, too their acquaintance.

We talk sometimes, my auto pilot and I,
It assures me tomorrow will be the same,
A frequent trip of normality,
As for today, my auto pilot did it's job well,
And I, it's passenger successfully reached my destination,
The end of another day.

# LOUD SCREAMS

Why can no one hear it?
These screams abhorrently loud;
I flinch from their deafening pitch,
But no one hears a sound.

It's so hard to remain focussed,
Such chaos deep within;
I crave for simple silence,
Why must peace be such a sin?

It's hard to hear people talking,
Above these cries of utter despair;
So why can no one hear it,
I wonder if they care.

# THINGS I'LL NEVER BE

I think of fearless warriors,
Sword and shield in hand;
A heroic sense of purpose,
As they make their final stand.

I think of being successful,
And the confidence that will bring;
Life's simpler when you have,
I'll want for not a thing.

I think of a companion,
Who understands my pain;
They'll take away my demons,
A soulmate I shall gain.

I think of being a role model,
Inspiring those in need;
Whomever be in desperate search for hope
I'll help them plant the seed.

I think of being healed,
I think of being free;
I think of all these things,
These things I'll never be.

# SUNSHINE & RAINBOWS

The world is sunshine and rainbows,
A lie we often tell;
More the absence of a heaven,
Trapped in Dante's hell.

Dark and ruthless monsters,
None more so than my own mind;
They cloud the warmth and light
More powerful over time.

A land of opportunity,
Prosper shall the brave;
But I am not life's citizen,
I'm merely but it's slave.

A surround of beauty and splendour they say,
Take wonder in the stars;
But they are well beyond me,
Out of reach a step too far.

The world in sunshine and rainbows,
To some so it may seem;
For me a little bleaker,
Even absent from my dreams.

# KALEIDOSCOPE

My world, the kaleidoscope;
Reality changing with each turn,
Continuously folding into the next chaotic scene;
Often full of spectacular beauty and splendour,
Of which my mind cannot make sense.

# I WONDER IF THEY KNOW

I wonder if they know,
My life is all a show;
Nothing that is real,
Hiding how I feel.

I wonder if they see,
That it's not the real me;
Who listens whilst they speak,
Inside secretly weak.

I wonder is it real,
The darkness that I feel;
Always feeling low,
I wonder if they know.

# BATTLEFIELD

In the battlefield of my own thoughts,
At my enemy's mercy,
The enemy that is me;
A conflict with no resolution,
Forever in mortal danger.

A mind at war.

# THE AFFLICTED

The afflicted;
Chosen without a choice,
Criers without a voice,
A twisting ache of chaos.

# MY ANCHOR

My anchor,
Keeping me tied to this world,
Preventing me from drifting away;
Through the darkest storms,
And the calmest seas,
I'm always here,
Where you can always find me,
In the safety of your harbour;
And whilst you're attached,
I'll never drift away.

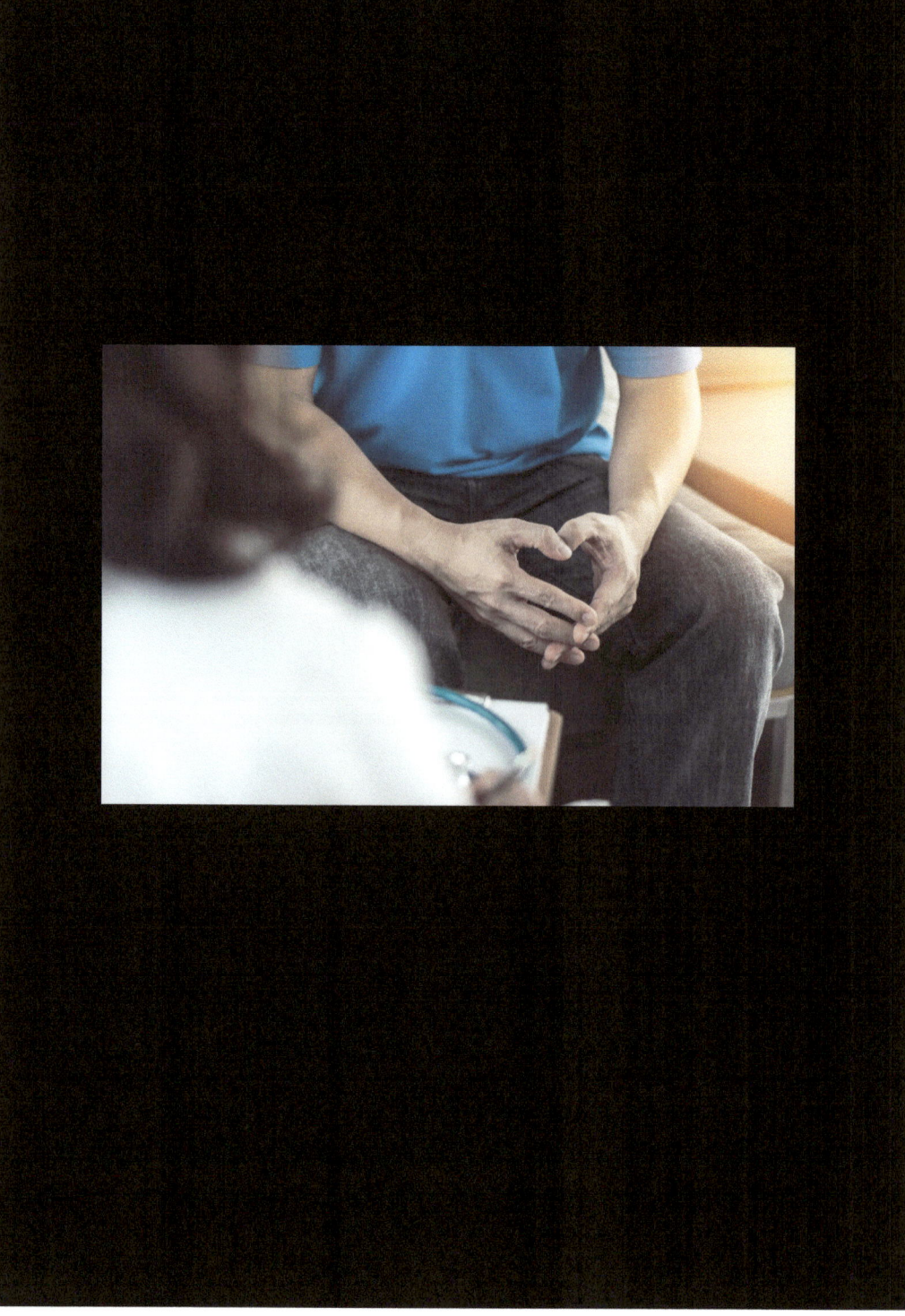

# THE COUNSELLOR

Our position is symbolic,
We sit at opposite ends;
You not understanding,
Pretending we are friends.

And still you cannot know me,
However you may try;
I'm forced to share my pain,
But you will not tell me why.

I say that it is helping,
Horrors you force me to relive;
So ask another question,
But I've not much more to give.

A certificate of understanding,
Qualified to put on a show;
But however many times you listen to us,
You don't feel it, so you can't know.

We sit at opposite ends,
And that is all I know.

# WOULD YOU STILL LOVE ME

I wonder if you'd still love me,
If you saw the real me;
If you looked a little closer,
If I let you in to see.

Would you still think me your hero,
If you knew all there was to know;
Would you hold my heart so gently,
Or would you turn away and go.

Would you embrace me as a soulmate,
Or would you be afraid;
If you were part of all my suffering,
Would you leave and I be blamed.

So tell me would you still love,
Knowing mind and heart are ill;
If you truly knew me,
Could you love me still?

# ANGRY BEAR CUB

Angry bear cub,
Full of rage,
Trapped within a mortal cage.

A contradiction,
Full of grace,
Wrapped with an angelic face.

Perform for masters,
Must be good,
Heard but never understood.

Unworldly beauty,
Out of place,
My angry bear cub,
Full of grace.

# THE BOXING RING OF LIFE

Life is like a boxing ring.

We enter pure, prepared and ready,
Knowing that whatever happens,
We're going to come out damaged in some way.
The low blows take our breath away.
We cling tightly to what hurts us,
Believing that in an enemy's embrace we're safe.
Never more than a few feet,
From those that mean us harm.
Everyone that loves us,
Forced to watch from the outside.
That ever growing temptation,
To go down when we get hit hard.
But not wanting to let down,
Those that built us up.
The ever-inviting warmth of the canvas,
Signalling the end of the struggle,
Of fighting for your life in every round.

But alas, you are a fighter.
So hold on,
Fight back,

Survive.

# PRIME OF LIFE

Middle aged and far from prime,
Glory of a different time;
Best achievements in the past,
Invincibility that didn't last.

Joints that ache and bones that creek,
Sturdy shoulders falling weak;
Remembering of a different time,
Agile, nimble, in your prime.

But Father Time it also gave,
Beloved children misbehave;
I wouldn't change a single hair,
Child's beauty beyond compare.

A life companion offered too,
A lonely wolf became a few;
Starting glories of anew,
Love and friendship true.

So middle aged and far from prime,
Appreciate the current time;
Enjoy all that you have today,
'Cause time will take it all away.

# SILENT RAGE

I'm patient in a queue
*GET OUT MY FUCKING WAY!*

I'm passive when abused
*WHAT DID YOU FUCKING SAY!*

I'm quiet in a crowd
*I'D LOVE TO KILL YOU ALL!*

I'm supportive to a fault
*I HOPE YOU FUCKING FALL!*

Protective of my soul
*HOW DARE YOU FUCKING CRY!*

A real zest for life
*I WANT TO FUCKING DIE!*

# CHAOTIC AMUSEMENT

Anarchy and clarity,
A contradicting hilarity,
A widening disparity,
Between reality and my own sanity.

# A SPECIAL SIBLING

It tortures me to know,
That over time you'll fade;
The rose will lose its petals,
Encompassed by the shade.

Fate it can be cruel,
Without mercy it can choose;
The least deserving of a sibling,
To twist, torture and abuse.

Unable to trade places,
For momentary release;
To quieten your demons,
For a life filled only with peace.

A smile that's always full of hope,
Resilience that inspires;
Protecting those around you first,
Nurturing their desires.

I wish that you could see,
Your spirit shines brighter every day;
And that you'll always be my hero,
In every single way,

Forever your big brother,
I'll never go away.


"Never give up, little one.  You're my hero xx"

# KARA

Brightest diamond in the sky,
Twilight beauty passed us by,
You chose to leave,
we don't know why,
And every day we cry.

A worldly angel gone too soon,
A new companion for the moon;
You took your place amongst the stars,
Now forced to love you from afar.

Regretful torment haunts us still,
Guilty suffering makes us ill;
Why couldn't you have just reached out,
Made us listen, scream and shout.

Visiting where you were laid to rest,
Grieving how we know the best;
Glossy marble holds your face,
Your new home and special place.

So watch over loved ones from afar,
But please leave heaven's door ajar;
And I'll join you there when it's time,
And everything will be just fine,
When once again I'm yours and you're mine.

My bright diamond in the sky.

# A DIFFERENT PATH

If fate had meant me different,
A sweeter path to tread;
A journey full of kindness,
A painless road instead.

A quest amongst companions,
Not a yard alone to take,
We'd go uphill together,
Get over our mistakes.

If fate had meant me different,
How better life could be;
A mind that's not so cloudy,
A calm and tranquil sea.
It just wasn't meant to be.

If fate had blessed me with a courage,
That shows how to survive;
If fate had meant me different.
I may still be alive.

If you need help, reach out…


Samaritans (UK):

116 123

24 hours a day/7 days a week


National Suicide Prevention Lifeline (USA):

1-800-273-8255

24 hours a day/7 days a week

www.ingramcontent.com/pod-product-compliance
Ingram Content Group UK Ltd.
Pitfield, Milton Keynes, MK11 3LW, UK
UKHW050927250325
5141UKWH00020B/83